Cycling

The sport of cycling has many variations and has something to offer for everyone. This book explores the whole range and illustrates the sport with colour photographs of both the top international stars and children in action.

InterSport

Cycling

Ken Evans

Colour photographs by All-Sport Limited

Wayland/Silver Burdett

InterSport

The world of international sport seen
through the cameras of some of the world's
greatest sports photographers, showing in
action both children and the stars they
admire.

Basketball   On Horseback
Cycling   Snow Sports
Golf   Soccer
Gymnastics   Swimming and Diving
Ice Sports   Tennis
Motorcycling   Track and Field

Frontispiece: **A bunch of the best** – A group of the
world's top racing stars, Michel Pollentier, Dietrich
Thurau and Joop Zoetemelk among them, claw their way
up a hill, cheered on by the crowd lining the route.

First published in 1980 by Wayland Publishers Limited
49 Lansdowne Place, Hove, East Sussex BN3 1HF, England
© Copyright 1980 Wayland Publishers Limited
ISBN 0 85340 772 X

Published in the United States by Silver Burdett Company, Morristown, New Jersey
1980 Printing
ISBN 0–382 06427–5

Phototypeset by Trident Graphics Limited, Reigate, Surrey
Printed in Italy by G. Canale & C.S.p.A., Turin

Contents

Introduction

Millions of people all over the world, many of them children, own bicycles. Cycling is an enjoyable pastime. It is a pleasant way to get to school or work every day, and it is one of the cheapest forms of transport. It keeps you fit too!

Cycling is also a major international sport. Men, women and even children can race against each other using their strength and any number of tactics to win.

Racing began about a century ago in France where the Tour de France, the world's most famous cycling event, still takes place every year. Interest grew in Italy and Belgium and these three countries were soon producing top cyclists. They allowed racing to take place on the roads, even closing certain roads to other traffic so that a race could take place undisturbed. Road racing became a professional sport, and any boy in France, Italy or Belgium with a bike knew that he could make a fortune if he trained hard enough.

Meanwhile things were very different in Britain. The authorities banned cycle racing

The will to win – Gianbatista Barronchelli grits his teeth and wills his machine to the summit of a climb during the Tour of Italy.

The greatest stage race – The Tour de France is the most gruelling and famous bicycle race held anywhere in the world. Here riders snake their way up the Col du Galibibe.

9

The end in sight – A group of riders who have 'broken away' from the main bunch, jockey for position before the final sprint towards the line during a stage of the Tour of Belgium.

from the roads. So cycle enthusiasts did not get the practice they badly needed, and the sport did not gain many fans. It was not until the 1970s that interest in road racing grew in Britain, and young riders were truly encouraged. On the track, however, British riders did better. Britain's most famous cyclist is Reg Harris, who was five times World Sprint Champion in the 1940s and 1950s.

In America, too, cycling did not become popular until the 1970s, though it had been introduced at the turn of the century. Ameri-

Out of the saddle – The rider up the banking is about to turn on the power during a 1000 m sprint race against Reg Harris.

cans have always had hard tracks in their country on which professional international events take place, but road racing did not catch on. British and American racers have to go to Europe for road races, where they are well established. And sometimes, a rider from Britain, America, Holland, Germany or Switzerland beats a champion among the French, Italians and Belgians.

Cycling clubs

Cycling means freedom! You can go where you want on your bicycle, stopping off when and where it pleases you. You can go as fast as you want, or pedal slowly along and enjoy the scenery. Experienced riders can go up to 160 kilometres (100 miles) in a day without difficulty. It just depends on how far your legs and your heart will carry you.

For many people, this is all they want from cycling. But if you are more serious about cycling, or want companionship from it, joining a club is the next step. You *have* to belong to a club if you want to race. Most clubs have coaches who train riders for the events they would like to compete in – anything from a sprint round the track to 12-hour or even 24-hour time trials where the object is to travel as far as you can within the time. Perhaps eventually you can become a member of a club racing team and this can be a thrilling experience.

Cycling clubs are also for tourists – people who ride purely for pleasure. Most clubs have a regular 'club run' at weekends. This is a day's ride with stops for lunch and tea.

A well earned rest – Time for a picnic beside a country road in Somerset, England.

The pace is set by the slowest rider, and no one is trying to get anywhere in a hurry. Sometimes the club has a weekend away, stopping at a youth hostel or small hotel overnight.

For the less experienced cyclist who is not ready for competition, club riding is a good way to learn how to handle your bicycle properly, how to use the gears, how to judge pace and how to climb hills and come down the other side in the correct manner. These

A more leisurely pace – Cycling is not all speed, crowds and glamour – it is also a very pleasant way to travel! Here we can see a group of cyclists preparing their bikes before setting off from a Youth Hostel in Yorkshire, England.

The freedom of the road – No road tax, no fuel bills, just carefree travel for this group of cyclists.

are skills that a racing cyclist must possess, and many racers use club runs as useful training sessions, especially during the winter months.

More experienced riders at the club will tell you about bike maintenance – how to keep your bike in top condition and how to repair it if it breaks down.

Racing bikes

Many bicycle manufacturers use the term 'racing bike' for any machine with dropped handlebars and 5-, 10- or 12-speed gears. But true racing bikes can rarely be found in the manufacturers' catalogues. Instead they are put together by the racer himself, buying whichever components he finds are best for him as an individual.

The modern racing bike is very light, weighing only 9 kg (20 lb). The handlebars, wheel rims, gear mechanisms and chain-wheels are all made from light but strong metal alloys. Racing machines must be light so that they can go fast. But they cannot be made completely from alloys, because a strong structure is necessary to bear the rider's weight. So the frame tubing on which the rest of the bike is assembled is still made of steel, though this steel is not much thicker than an eggshell.

A road machine has 10 or 12 gear ratios, which makes hill-climbing easier and also allows the racer to take advantage of the strongest tailwinds. You need a low gear to go uphill and a high gear to go downhill if

The track machine – Eddy Merckx powers over the boards on his light track cycle. Notice the fixed wheels and the absence of brakes.

you are to save your energy. Wheels can be removed by quickly flicking levers on the hub, so little time is lost if you puncture your tyre during a race and have to fit a new tyre or wheel.

The tyres themselves are very special. They are called tubulars or 'tubs'. They are very different from normal tyres which have inner tubes fitted separately inside the outer covers. The outer section of the tubular is sewn around a very light inner tube and the whole thing is stuck by a special glue to the rim. A tubular tyre can be removed and a new one fitted by the roadside in a minute or so – an obvious advantage when you want to get back into the race quickly.

A track machine is even lighter than a road racing bike. It weighs about 7 kg (16 lb). It has only one gear, and that is a 'fixed-wheel' type. This means that the pedal cranks must turn whenever the back wheel does. You can use the fixed-wheel system for slowing down – which is just as well as this machine has no brakes!

A racing bike will cost at least £250, ($500) and could cost three times as much if the best accessories are used. The best idea is to buy a bike with a good frame and then improve the accessories as you can afford to.

The road machine – Eddy Merckx's favourite road machine can here be seen leaning up against the team's car (left).

The all-surface machine – Cyclo-cross bikes are sturdier than road racing machines, as they have to be ridden and carried through mud, over fields and along forest paths.

19

Road racing

Road races take place on ordinary roads that are either closed to other traffic or chosen because little traffic uses them. The courses run from town to town or on a circuit that is covered several times by the riders, so that the spectators see the race pass by more than once.

Some circuits are in town centres and take only about two minutes to cover. These are the best events if you want to see plenty of action and high-speed cornering.

In road racing, competitors start together and the first rider to cross the finishing-line will be the winner. But this does not mean that everyone sprints away from the start as hard as possible – far from it. Tactics play a big part, for strength and energy need to be saved for the final sprint.

The best way to save your strength during the race is to use the tactic 'slipstreaming'. This means riding behind another rider, using him as shelter from the wind. Riding in a big group is better than riding on your own or in a small bunch, as you can take most advantage of slipstreaming.

The massed start – The start of a road race can sometimes be hazardous. One pedal getting caught up in another rider's wheel can start a chain reaction leading to a mass crash!

Many races are for individuals, but some are for teams which can contain from three to a dozen riders. Usually after the halfway point in the race, one rider may break away as the riders go round a corner or climb a hill, perhaps. This is taking a gamble as the rider loses the shelter of the big group, but he has the element of surprise on his side. If more than one rider breaks away, they may start 'working' which means taking turns to ride at the front and shelter the others. The breakaway team may draw steadily clear and gain the lead, hoping that the bunch behind will be too disorganized by this sudden tactic to catch up. If the team has a star sprinter in its midst, then the other members of the team will shelter him so that he can save his energy. The star man may break away on his own at any favourable time in the race, and make a sprint for the finishing-line.

Setting the pace – This leading rider forces the pace in the hope that she will be able to 'break away' from her pursuers.

Getting a 'tow' – Tactics play a very great part in most forms of cycle racing. This rider is not really hanging on to the rider in front but riding in his slipstream . . . a tactic which enables him to save energy (left).

Stage races

The toughest road races are the 'stage' races. They are called stage races because the course is split up into daily stages.

The most famous stage race is the Tour de France. The word 'tour' has nothing to do with touring, it is the French word for a circuit. But this circuit is not like the town centre circuits mentioned in the last chapter. The Tour de France is a circuit which runs for the incredible distance of 4000 kilometres (2500 miles). Not many of us could manage a circuit of that length, but the professionals cover it in four weeks. The Tour de France is the greatest event of the cycling calendar and riders come from all over the world to compete.

Each daily stage of a marathon like this is a race in itself. Riders are timed each day and the one with the shortest time to his credit is the winner for that stage. The rider with the shortest time over all stages wears a distinctive yellow jersey, and other specially-coloured jerseys are worn by the best mountain climber, best finishing sprinter, and so on. Riders reach speeds of

The British Milk Race – Over the last few years, cycling has become ever more popular in Britain. The most important stage race, held each year, is the Milk Race. Here, Phil Edwards leads Nickson and Kowalski.

TO25052

25

40 km/h (25 mph) on the flat and sometimes up to twice that speed when descend-
ing mountain passes.

Imitations of the Tour de France take
place in Spain and Italy, two other great
cycling countries. The organizers of these
stage races change the routes every year and
try to find the right mixture of flat road,

The price of success – No rider, no matter
how brilliant a cyclist, can hope to win a stage
race without the very expensive support of his
team.

Legs of steel – A stage race cyclist, like Jiri
Bartolsic of Czechoslovakia, must have
incredible strength and stamina if he is to
survive a gruelling Tour (right).

mountains and rough surfaces to produce a winner who can master any kind of course.

Racing for such long periods of time would be impossible without the help of skilled officials. Each team has its own mechanics, masseur, and manager. During the race, team service cars carrying spare bikes and wheels in case of punctures and breakdowns follow their riders, and often the manager in the team car will shout instructions to his riders.

In the Continental tours all the professional riders are sponsored by commercial companies, whose names they wear on their jerseys.

The star of stage racing in the 1970s was Eddy Merckx of Belgium, winner of five Tour de France races and five Tours of Italy.

Britain's longest stage race is the Milk Race, but unlike the Continental tours it is for amateur riders only. It lasts about twelve days and is for six- or seven-man teams from different countries.

Follow the leader – Eddy Merckx (yellow jersey) leads the Tour de France. The incredible Merckx won no less than five Tour de France races!

Time trialling

'Mass start' racing had to be abandoned in Britain at the turn of the century because of objections by the police. So British cyclists invented the sport of time trialling, which is still popular today in Britain, though it is rarely practised on the Continent.

Instead of starting in a bunch as road racers do, time triallists are started at one-minute intervals. Sometimes one rider will catch another, but the rule is that the over-taken rider must not take shelter in the slipstream of the overtaker. So trials involve 'unpaced' riding – this means you cannot use another rider to help you decide how fast to go. There are no tactics. The rider with the fastest time wins.

Courses are carefully measured and are usually on some form of circuit or else they are 'out and home' – which means there is a turning-point that leads you back along the same route to the finish. There are also place-to-place trials. Marshals stand at intervals along the route to point the way and to check each rider is following the proper route. Other helpers hand up

Giving his all – John Patston of Great Britain knows only too well what the right speed is for a time trial – as fast as humanly possible!

30

refreshments and sponges to riders as they swoop past – after several hours of running a hundred yards up the road to retrieve a discarded sponge or plastic bottle, rushing back to refill it, and handing it up to the next rider, helpers often get as much exercise as the riders!

Most races are over standard distances of 25, 50 and 100 miles. You also get 12 and 24 hour races which finish on a circuit. They start very early in the morning – at dawn sometimes – so you have to be up early if you want to see them. The event usually ends with all the riders, marshals, and time-keepers going off to have breakfast together! There are special events for schoolchildren under 16, for juniors under 18, and for veterans over 40.

'Opens' are trials which are open to people outside the club. They include the 12 and 24 hour 'mile-eaters' and are contested by up to 120 riders. Of course many officials have to be present to check distances and times and keep control.

The great thing about time trialling is that you don't have to be brilliant. You go out to beat your own 'personal best'. To enter opens, you just need a roadworthy machine – so this is an ideal start for beginners in Britain.

Against the clock – A time triallist, like Joachim Agostinho here, must be capable of judging his own speed (left).

The lone rider – Nothing in sight but the open road. In a time trial, the rider is very much out on his own!

Track racing

Cycling tracks have surfaces of concrete, asphalt or hardwood. They are roughly oval in shape and usually have banked curves. Lap distances can be anything from 160 m (175 yds) to 500 m (547 yds). A popular size is 333 m (364 yds). This is the size of the Leicester track in England where the 1982 World Cycling Championships will be held.

In most track events, races start with all riders setting off together for a race of many laps, using much the same tactics as road racing. But in sprint events, strange-looking tactics come into play, with each rider (usually two or three) trying to stay behind the others for as long as possible. This is to take advantage of the slipstreaming. You will often see the front rider slowing down or even standing still, balancing his bicycle for minutes at a time, trying to tempt his opponent into the lead. Because of these cat-

Manoeuvring for position – Two riders playing cat and mouse in the early stages of a sprint race.

The team slipstream – The first rider in a pursuit team 'tows' his team mates round the banked circuit as fast as he can before dropping back to let another member take over (left).

and-mouse tactics, times for sprint races are taken over the last 200 metres only, when positioning no longer matters and everyone is making a dash for the line. Sometimes a rider will maximize his speed by swooping down from the top of the curve.

In pursuit events, riders or teams of riders chase each other. They start on opposite sides of the track and if one catches the other, victory is theirs. Otherwise it is the rider or team with the fastest time over the distance who wins. 'Devil take the Hindmost'

Up the banking – In team pursuit races, the team of four work for each other to ensure the fastest possible time. Victory is decided on the times of the first three racers in each team. Here we can see a member of the team swoop up the banking to allow a team mate to take the lead.

Tracking the machine – Motorcycles used in pacing must have a 500 cc to 1000 cc engine. They must also have a roller projecting behind the rear wheel to prevent a serious accident should the cyclist's front wheel touch it.

(also called 'Miss-and-Outs' and 'Elimination' in different parts of the world) is a race of skill. The last rider across the line every lap or couple of laps is eliminated, and the final lap is fought out between the two riders left.

The fastest of all track races are motor-cycle-paced. The track rider uses a much larger gear than normal as he is racing in the slipstream of a motorcycle. It is possible to achieve an average speed of 80 km/h (50 mph). The field usually consists of six or eight riders, each with his own motorcycle pacer.

A typical track meeting will last an afternoon or an evening and will contain many of these different track events.

Six-day racing

The most spectacular form of cycle racing is the six-day race. It takes place during the winter on indoor tracks. It started in America but now mostly takes place in Europe, with the West Germans being its most ardent supporters.

Once six-day races were gruelling endurance tests for individual riders. But it was no fun for spectators to watch riders trying to keep awake and getting slower and slower. So the current formula is to have two-man (and sometime three-man) teams. Each team races for only a few hours each day. Six-day racing shows off the skills of the riders in the sprints, Devils and bunched races and is always thrilling to watch.

Various events are held within the six days of racing. The most important is the Madison race (named after Madison Square Garden, the sports stadium in New York where the event became popular). A Madison is a continuous relay. One team member races flat out for a lap or two while his partner rests on the outer section of the track. When it is the other man's turn, the

The track racing circuit – This picture, taken in Ghent, Belgium, captures the feeling of 'enclosed speed' experienced by riders on a banked circuit.

racing rider grabs his team-mate's trailing hand and slings him forward into action. The aim is to gain ground on the other teams and if one team leads by a lap at the end of the six-day programme, it is an outright win. If teams are level on the lap-counts, then points gained in other events decide the winner.

The world's greatest six-day rider is Patrick Sercu of Belgium, who achieved victory for the seventieth time in 1980, a world record.

The hand-over – In Six-day racing, one member of the two-man team races flat out for a lap or two before literally handing over to his team mate. Jan Raas and Gerrie Knetteman show how it's done.

Cyclo-cross

Not all winter racing takes place on indoor circuits. Most of it is outside, through natural hazards such as mud, ice and snow. It is called cyclo-cross and it is great fun. Most events take entries 'on the line' so you can just turn up with your bike, with no advance entry necessary. There are events for adults and children.

Cyclo-cross is cross-country racing with a bicycle – ridden, dragged, or carried, according to the circumstances. You have to know just when it is no longer worth straining at the pedals up a muddy hill, and gauge the right moment to leap off, hoist the bicycle on to your shoulder, and start running.

For going through slippery mud, you will need a good sense of balance. You will also need plenty of stamina for the bike will become sluggish as it gets clogged with mud. You can get up speed on the fast stretches of road and smooth grassland, and a little daring goes a long way on steep gravelly descents. The best cyclo-cross riders combine sheer strength, lightness of build, skill and

About to descend – Cyclo-cross racers can reach almost frightening speeds on downhill stretches, even over very bumpy ground, as Chris Dodd demonstrates.

the courage to go as fast as the conditions allow.

Although you can go in for cyclo-cross on an ordinary bicycle, top riders' bikes are different. They are like road machines that have been altered to suit this type of racing. The bikes have five or ten gears but gear ratios are wider – you need a very low gear to force your way through thick mud, yet most courses include fast stretches. There is a guard to stop the chain jumping off as you bump over really rough areas. Wheels have heavier spokes and the tyres, whilst still racing tubulars, have a knobbly tread for improved grip. Frames are designed with plenty of ground clearance so that the chain and hubs do not become completely clogged with mud. In major races, riders change bikes once or twice during each lap. Helpers stand by to clean off the mud with a hose while the other bike is in use.

Usually races go on for about an hour, although races for children are less than half-an-hour of frenzied activity. There are usually several events at each meeting.

Cycle racing? – In cyclo-cross, it is sometimes quicker to get off your bike and carry it, than to attempt to ride it!

Training

Like many truly athletic sports, cycle racing demands hours of dedicated training each week. Even track sprinters, whose event might last only a minute or so, need to cover many kilometres in training.

Young people are usually quite fit because of school sports, and this is a good basis for cycle training. You should not think of training for special distances or events but just practise regularly on the bike.

Strangely enough, many cyclists hardly touch their bikes during the winter months. They prefer to give themselves a rest from cycling. However, they are far from being idle during this period. Top riders choose another sport to keep themselves in trim, like squash or badminton, or perhaps cross-country running.

Top cyclists often include weight training in their winter programme. The purpose of training with weights is to build up those muscles which are neglected in cycling – especially those in the top half of the body. Many also try circuit training, which involves doing exercises which work all the

A break in the training – As in any sport, the harder you train, the better you will become.

body's muscles and build up the heart.

As the racing season approaches, out come the bikes again and steady bike riding becomes the main activity. Cycling in low gears at first encourages good pedalling action. As the weather gets warmer, mature riders can include some 'interval training'. This is tough training involving flat-out sprints with intervals of 'resting' – then another sprint. This is very demanding, and all the body-training during winter should now pay off.

This is the winter programme for a star rider. But, young people just need to ride as often as possible throughout the year, including the winter, so that pedalling and handling the machine become second nature.

Cycle racing for young riders

You don't have to be an adult before you can race on a bicycle – or become a world champion for that matter. Most countries have some kind of racing programme for youngsters who are not yet physically mature but whose urge to compete is fully developed!

In Britain, for example, competition for boys is divided into schoolboy (under-16) and junior (under-18) categories, with similar racing for girls too. The English Schools' Cycling Association runs a long list of championships from tourist competitions to racing. The British Cycling Federation (BCF) handles road and track racing and the Road Time Trials Council (RTTC) runs time trials. Both of these have schoolboy and junior racing programmes and work together to produce a joint coaching scheme.

If you're under 16, you won't be able to race on public roads unless you are doing a time trial on a safe course. But you can race on cycle tracks or on closed-road circuits such as the specially-built 1.6 km Eastway circuit,

The thrill of competition – These youngsters are experiencing competition in the right surroundings – a track far away from motorised vehicles.

close to Stratford in East London. For track and road racing, there are rules to restrict the gearing you can use to encourage you to pedal faster rather than push harder.

The British Cycling Federation runs several national championships for schoolboys and juniors. The circuit and road events are held in different parts of the country each year, but the track championships are held at an annual nine-day championship meeting at Leicester, along with all the senior title racing.

From the age of 17, boys can race in the World Junior Championship series. This covers track and road events and is held in a different country each year, staged just like the senior World Championships. In 1979, the World Road Race Championship for women was won by a Dutch girl called Petra de Bruin, who was only just 17. Girls need only be 16 to ride in this event.

So you don't have to wait until you can vote before you can race. Young teenagers aren't just welcome – they're encouraged.

All Hail the conquering hero! – Everyone loves to be the victor, but it must never be forgotten that competing in a sport is just as important as winning.

The younger you start . . . This young lady is already well on the way to becoming a very good cyclist. So the younger you can start, the better (left).

On the fringe

The cycle racing you have read about so far in this book is a bit different from the unofficial races you have with your friends around the neighbourhood. But two special types of racing have grown up from the kind of rough-riding times we have all had on local parks or common land. These are cycle speedway and BMX – bicycle moto-cross.

Cycle speedway is an imitation of motor-cycle speedway, ridden on short, tight tracks of dirt or cinders, with the emphasis on getting a fast start into the first bend and holding off all challengers if you can. It's highly organized – you can find clubs all over the country specializing in speedway, and matches between representative teams are held all through the summer.

It's quite easy to convert a bike for cycle speedway. A low gear to ensure a quick getaway from the starting gate, a pair of straight or cow-horn handlebars, and some tough tyres are the only essentials. Then it's just a matter of furious pedalling for the chance to outmanoeuvre your rivals.

BMX is a very recent 'invention', and

Airborne – Bicycle moto-cross can involve the rider in a number of spills – so it is always wise to wear protective clothing and a crash helmet.

although it is very popular in America, it has only just begun to catch on in Europe. Like motorcycling's moto-cross it takes place on rough circuits, and the emphasis is on bike-handling as much as on speed. A BMX bike has small wheels, cow-horn handlebars, a low gear, and some kind of springing or suspension to cushion the rider against the bumps of the course. The course hazards – sharp bends, ruts, switchbacks and mud-patches – are taken at full speed, and often star riders can be airborne as they sprint over the crest of a hill. It takes skill to make a good landing afterwards. The inevitable crashes mean that BMX riders usually sport knee and elbow protection as well as crash helmets and goggles. Although BMX is basically for very young riders, there are some well-paid professional teams in America whose skill in events is a good advertisement for this fast-growing form of cycle racing.

Rough riders! – Bicycle moto-cross is a variation of motorcycle moto-cross which can be enjoyed by youngsters.

T025052

Tourist trials

Not all forms of cycle competition are races. In many countries, non-racing cyclists stage their own events called tourist trials or standard rides. In France, cyclists who hold racing licences are not allowed to take part.

A tourist trial is a quiz on two wheels. In one type of trial riders follow a marked-out course across country. At any moment an official could step out from behind a tree to test their reaction, or to ask questions about various things the cyclist could have observed. Sometimes, the official keeps well hidden to watch the rider's handling of his bike over tricky sections.

Map-reading competitions are more difficult. The rider must find his way to various checkpoints using a large-scale map, and must answer questions either at each checkpoint or at the end of the ride. There is no high speed element in tourist trials, but a favourite test is to judge your speed, averaging a set speed over a few kilometres. Marks are lost if you travel faster or slower than the speed required.

Reliability trials usually take place

In search of solitude – A bicycle is perhaps the most peaceful way to get away from it all and enjoy the beauty of the countryside.

towards the end of winter. Riders are asked to complete a course in a chosen time. Eight hours for 160 kilometres (100 miles) is a common choice. This is not a race, as you are not allowed to finish more than a quarter of an hour within your set time; it is a test of steady riding.

In Europe, especially in France, long distance trials, sometimes going on for more than a day, are held on large circuits or from

The tourist trial – Tourist trials are an enjoyable test of a cyclist's all-round cycling awareness and ability. They stress the fact that cycling is, above all, fun.

place to place. One of the most popular is the Paris-Brest-Paris trial, which is held annually and is contested by more than 1000 riders from many countries. They set out to ride the distance inside a time standard of their own choice.

Time to go – A group of riders prepare for the start of a tourist trial.

Becoming a racing cyclist

If you want to become a Tour de France winner like Bernard Hinault of France, or a top track rider like Patrick Sercu of Belgium, then you have to make a good early start. The most important step is to join a cycling club. You can find the address at your local library or through friends. There may be several to choose from if you live in a large town. At the club you can start learning how to train, and how to handle your bike and keep it in good mechanical condition. You need lots of practice before you can compete with experienced riders.

Through the club you become an affiliated member of your national governing body of racing (at a cheap rate if you are still at school). To enter time trials you fill out an entry form at your club about two weeks before the event. But to compete in road and track racing, which may be run by the national governing body, you need a licence and you fill out a form for the national governing body. There may be restrictions in

A rough road to the top – Here a group of world-class cyclists negotiate a stretch of cobbled road during the Paris – Roubaix Classic. Dietrich Thurau leads from Freddy Maertens.

your country which mean that you must wait till you are 12 until you can race, and even then you must have the written consent of your parents or guardian.

Probably the easiest events to enter are cyclo-cross races for schoolchildren. You don't need a licence and you can usually enter on the day. But before you start racing, it is as well to put in plenty of riding practice, handling your bike on different types of road and in all sorts of weather. Cycle touring will help you to do this. And when choosing your races, don't go for long distance first. For under-16s, circuit events are usually about 17 km (10 miles) or less, and this is fine. Time trials can be between 17 and 40 km (10–25 miles) and it's best to stick to the shortest distances to begin with.

See you on the road!

The pick of the bunch – Bernard Hinault of France is thought by many to be the greatest cyclist in the world today.

Index

All pictures by All-Sport Photographic Ltd. except on pages 12, 14, 15, 56, 58 and 59 (Peter Knottley), and page 48 (Sports Plus).